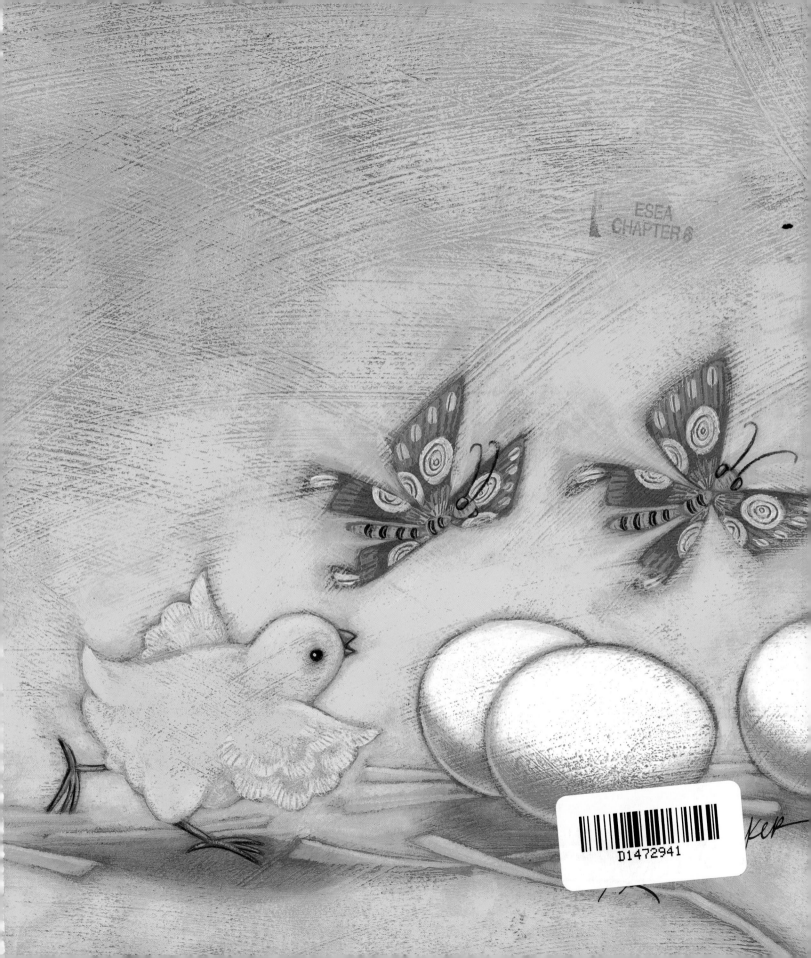

# Big Dreams

**Senior Authors**

Roger C. Farr

Dorothy S. Strickland

**Authors**

Richard F. Abrahamson ♦ Alma Flor Ada ♦ Barbara Bowen Coulter
Bernice E. Cullinan ♦ Margaret A. Gallego
W. Dorsey Hammond
Nancy Roser ♦ Junko Yokota ♦ Hallie Kay Yopp

**Senior Consultant**

Asa G. Hilliard III

**Consultants**

V. Kanani Choy ♦ Lee Bennett Hopkins ♦ Stephen Krashen ♦ Rosalia Salinas

# Harcourt Brace & Company

Orlando  Atlanta  Austin  Boston  San Francisco  Chicago  Dallas  New York  Toronto  London

Requests for permission to make copies of any part of the work should be mailed to: Permissions Department, Harcourt Brace & Company, 6277 Sea Harbor Drive, Orlando, Florida 32887-6777.

HARCOURT BRACE and Quill Design is a registered trademark of Harcourt Brace & Company.

Acknowledgments appear in the back of this work.

Printed in the United States of America

ISBN 0-15-306395-5

2 3 4 5 6 7 8 9 10   048   99 98 97

**Dear Reader,**

You'll find that the families of animals and people in this book have big wishes and dreams. They are a lot like you. Read the stories. Enjoy the poems. Meet all kinds of families like yours. **Big Dreams** can come from reading. So open up the book and follow your dreams.

Sincerely,

*The Authors*

The Authors

# ALL IN A FAMILY

# CONTENTS

# ALL IN A FAMILY

Special family times–which ones are the best? Share some fun with families as you read these stories.

# CONTENTS

# BOOKSHELF

## Five Little Monkeys Jumping on the Bed
by Eileen Christelow

A family of monkeys try to get a good night's sleep.

**Children's Choice**

SIGNATURES LIBRARY

## Vegetable Garden
by Douglas Florian

What kinds of seeds will a family plant to make their garden grow?

**Outstanding Science Trade Book for Children**

SIGNATURES LIBRARY

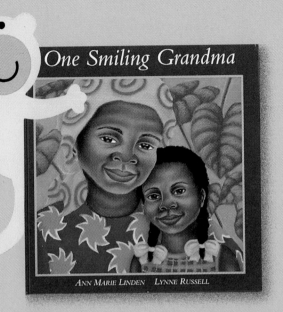

## One Smiling Grandma
by Ann Marie Linden

A girl finds many reasons to smile with her grandmother.

## Hide and Seek in the Yellow House
by Agatha Rose

Will Mother Cat ever find where her kitten, "Mack! Mack! Mack!" is hiding?

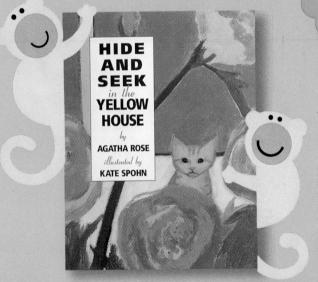

# An Egg Is An Egg
## by
## NICKI WEISS

An egg is an egg
Until it hatches.

And then it is a chick.

A branch is a branch
Until it breaks.

And then it is a stick.

Nothing stays the same.
Everything can change.

A seed is a seed
Until it is sown.

And then it is a flower.

A block is a block
Until there are many.

And then they become a tower.

Nothing stays the same.
Everything can change.

Water is water
Until it is brewed.

And then it becomes tea.

You are you
Until I come.

And then you become "we."

Nothing stays the same.
Everything can change.

The yard is green
Until it snows.

And then it becomes white.

Day is day
Until sunset.

And then it is the night.

Nothing stays the same.
Everything can change.

This baby was a baby
Until he grew.

And now he is a boy.

But you can always be a baby.

You will always be my baby....

Some things stay the same.
Some things never change.

# Nicki Weiss

Nothing stays the same for Nicki Weiss. Her life has been full of changes. She has lived in France, Jerusalem, and New York. She has been an artist, a bread baker, a school teacher, and now a writer. Did "An Egg Is An Egg" help you see the changes in your world?

# RESPONSE CORNER

## How did that happen?

Some things change all the time. Did you ever turn something old into something new? Now you can!

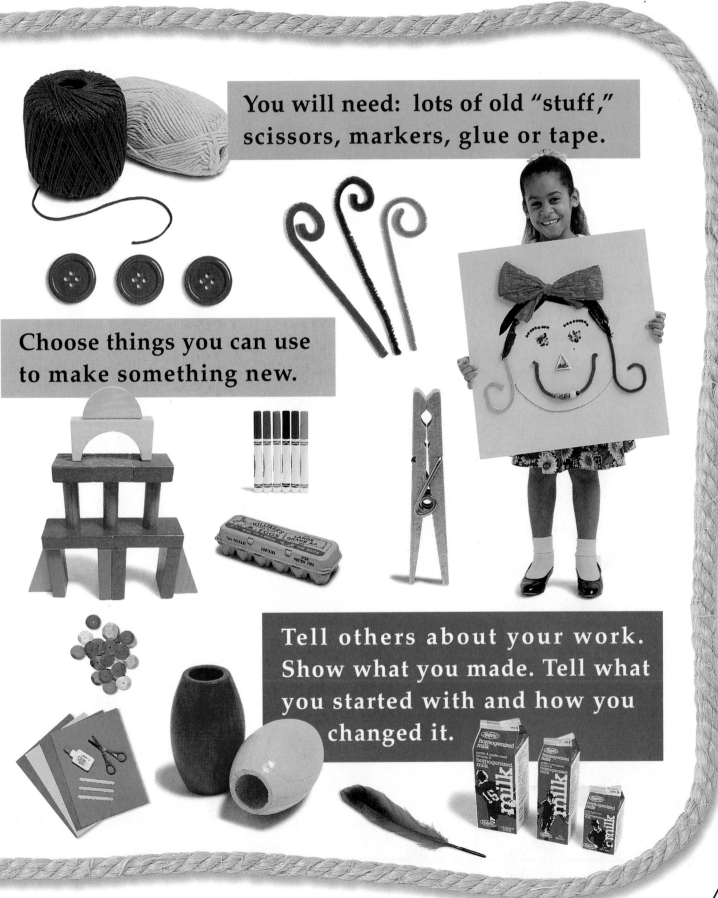

You will need: lots of old "stuff," scissors, markers, glue or tape.

Choose things you can use to make something new.

Tell others about your work. Show what you made. Tell what you started with and how you changed it.

# BET YOU CAN'T

## by PENNY DALE

45

55

59

# PENNY DALE

The two children in "Bet You Can't" seem very real. That's because Penny Dale likes to write about things that really happen to children. Often these children are her daughter, Sarah, and Sarah's friends.

Penny Dale says that sometimes just a few words from a boy or girl can give her an idea for a story. She makes the children she draws look like real children, too. She started drawing when she was a child herself.

# Where Did the

I cannot remember—
And neither can my mother—
Just when it was our baby
Turned into my brother.

# Baby Go?

by Julie Holder
illustrated by
Julia Gorton

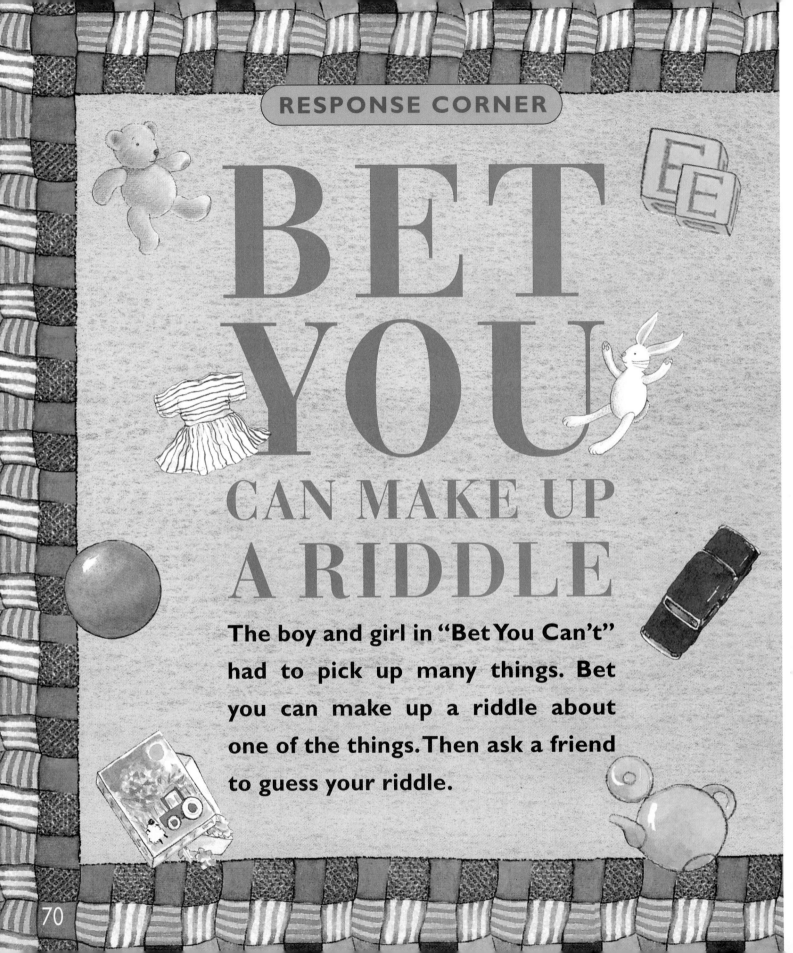

# BET YOU
## CAN MAKE UP
## A RIDDLE

The boy and girl in "Bet You Can't" had to pick up many things. Bet you can make up a riddle about one of the things. Then ask a friend to guess your riddle.

Pick something for your riddle.
Think of three things to say about it.
Ask someone to guess your riddle.
End your riddle with these words:
**BET YOU CAN'T GUESS!**

The toy has wheels.
It rolls. You wear it.
Bet you can't guess!

**NOW YOU CAN**

- *Write your riddle for a class book.*
- *Tape-record your riddle.*

# LITTLE ELEPHANT

photographs by **TANA HOBAN** story by **MIELA FORD**

Award-Winning Photographer

I am a little elephant.

This is my mother.
She lets me play in the water.

First one toe,

then two.

A big splash.
Lots of bubbles.

Up goes my trunk.

Swing it around.

Under I go.

Can you see me?

Here I am.
Time to get out.

This is hard.

Oops!

Can I make it?
Yes, I can!

Hurry now.

Where is my mother?

Waiting for me!

# TANA HOBAN

When I was a child, my father had a big camera. He took pictures as a hobby. Later my art teacher gave me a camera. It was just like the one my father had used! That's when I knew taking photos was for me. Now I carry a camera all the time.

I was happy when my daughter asked me if she could write the words for my book. Now this book is special to me because we worked together.

*Tana Hoban*

84

# MIELA FORD

I guess it's no surprise that I like to take pictures, too.
Both my mother and my father are photographers.
I had always wanted to work with
my mom. So I asked her if I could write
a story to go along with her photos.
Here's how I did it. I looked at the
pictures to see what story they
were telling me. The photos
told me "Little Elephant"!
Now I'm writing and
taking pictures for my own
books. My next one is
about bears.

*Miela Ford*

**W**ouldn't it be fun to make an album about the little elephant? Draw a picture of what you think the little elephant will do next. Write about your picture and put it in an album with others.

What can
I do next?

## Little Elephant's Album

Little elephant finds out how to squirt water.

**N**ow you can read and show the pages you made.

This **hare** is using its paws to wash its face.

This **bear** is bathing in a pond.

BATH

This **robin** is splashing in a bird bath.

This **ocelot** is licking its paws clean.

How do you take your bath?

TIME.

89

# Flower Garden

Written by
## Eve Bunting

Illustrated by
## Kathryn Hewitt

SHARED READING

Garden in a shopping cart
Doesn't it look great?

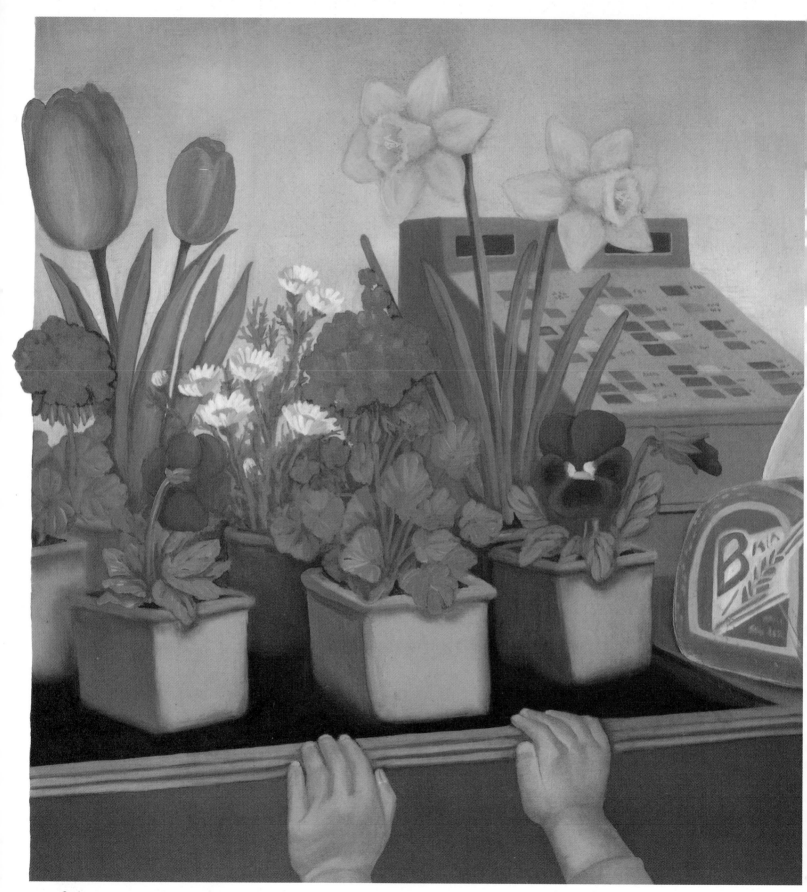

Garden on the checkout stand
I can hardly wait.

# Garden in a cardboard box
# Walking to the bus

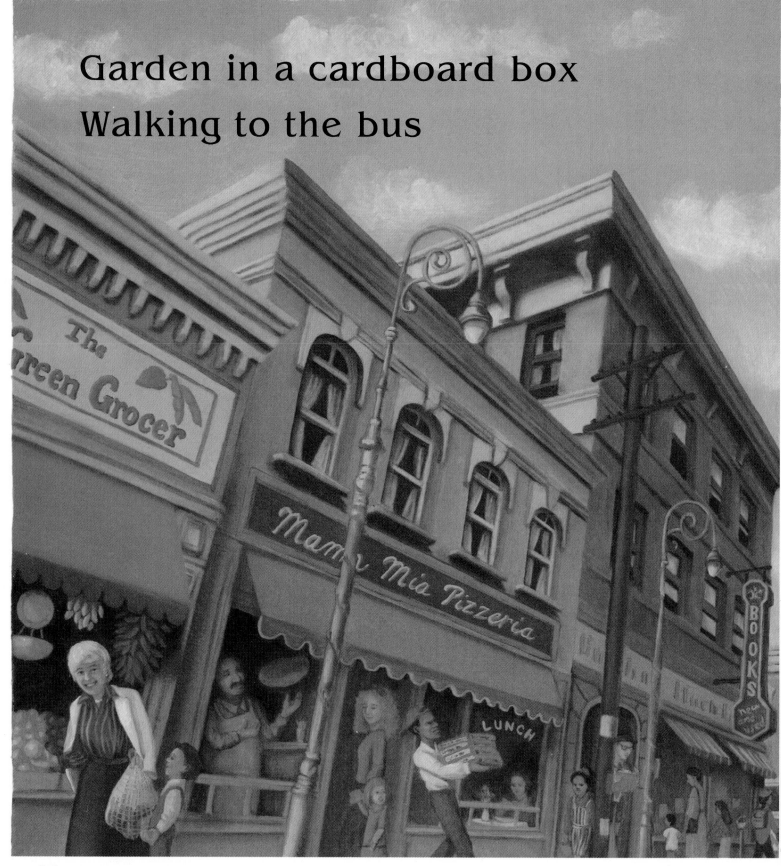

97

Garden sitting on our laps
People smile at us!

Garden going up the stairs
Stopping at each floor

This garden's getting heavier!
At last—our own front door.

Hurry! Hurry! Get the trowel
Spread the papers thick.

Get the bag of potting soil
Get the planting mix.

Put purple
pansies at
each end

Daisies, white
as snow

Daffodils,
geraniums,

and tulips,
in a row.

Garden in a window box
High above the street

Where butterflies
can stop and rest
And ladybugs can meet.

Walkers walking down below
Will lift their heads and see
Purple, yellow, red, and white
A color jamboree.

Candles on a birthday cake
Chocolate ice cream, too.

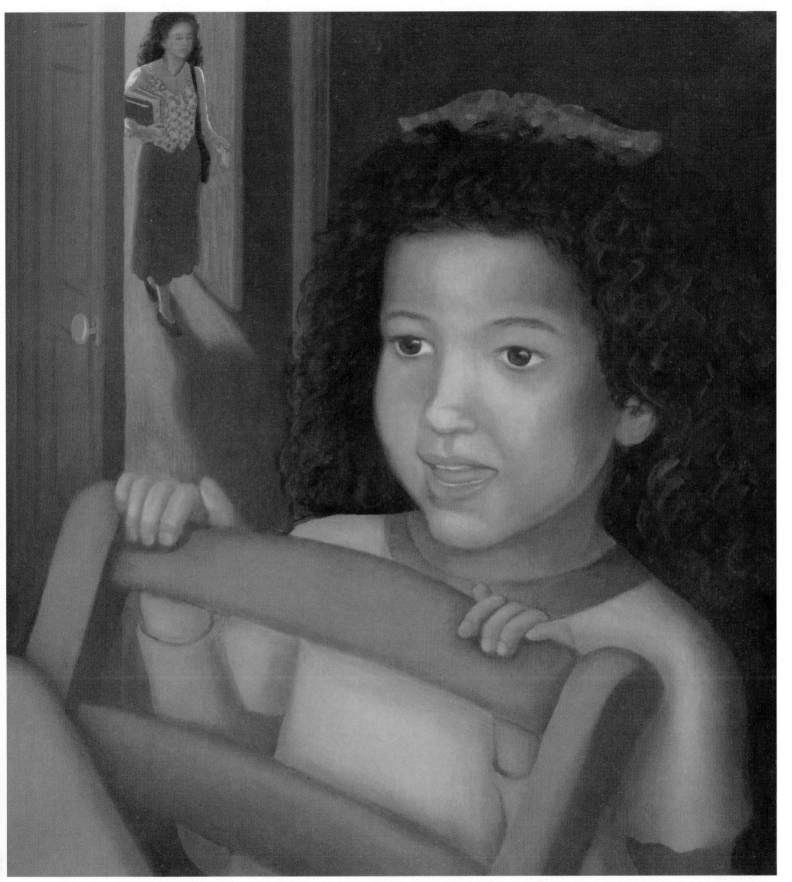

Happy, happy birthday, Mom!
A garden box—for you.

# Eve Bunting

## Growing Stories

My writing comes from things I've seen or heard. The thing to do if you want to write is to read and to love words. Keep a journal. Write just a few lines every day. Some day you will be happy to look back and read it.

*Eve Bunting*

# Kathryn Hewitt

## Growing Art

Before I started school, I drew all the time. If you draw something every day, at the end of the year, you will have 365 drawings. If you practice that much, you have to get better.

*Kathryn Hewitt*

# RESPONSE CORNER

How does your garden grow?

Kevin's garden

Roberto's gard

broccoli

zucchini

What kind of garden would you grow?
Show your plan. Draw a map of what you
will grow. Label the plants in each row.

1. Mark your spot on the mural.
2. Draw and label your garden.
3. Share your garden plan with classmates.
4. Talk about what all plants need to grow.

Amy's Garden

Radish

carrot

# Five Little
# DUCKS

·IAN·BECK·

Five little ducks went
swimming one day,
Over the hills and far away.

126

Mother duck said,

"Quack, quack, quack, quack."

But only four little ducks came back.

Four little ducks went swimming one day,
Over the hills and far away.

Mother duck said,

"Quack, quack, quack, quack."

But only three little ducks came back.

Three little ducks went swimming one day,
Over the hills and far away.

Mother duck said,
"Quack, quack, quack, quack."
But only two little ducks came back.

Two little ducks went swimming one day,
Over the hills and far away.

Mother duck said,
"Quack, quack, quack, quack."
But only one little duck came back.

133

One little duck went swimming one day,

Over the hills

and far away.

Mother duck said, "Quack, quack, quack, quack."

And all her five little ducks came back.

# ·IAN·BECK·

**Why did you retell this story about ducks?**

I love ducks. But I really told two stories in this book. One is the story of the ducks. The other is the story of the fox. I thought it would be fun to write a book that tells two stories at the same time.

**Why do you love ducks?**

When my daughter, Lily, was very small, her first word was *duck*. My wife, Emma, and I would take her and our sons for a stroll by the river. When Lily saw a bird in the water, she would point and say, "Duck." Now when I see a duck, it makes me smile.

*Ian Beck*

## Acting It Out

You can make a duck hat to wear. Then, you can quack, waddle, and act out the story of the ducks in "Five Little Ducks," or make up your own story to act out.

140

# You will need:

a paper plate • scissors • crayons • construction paper • glue • tape • stapler

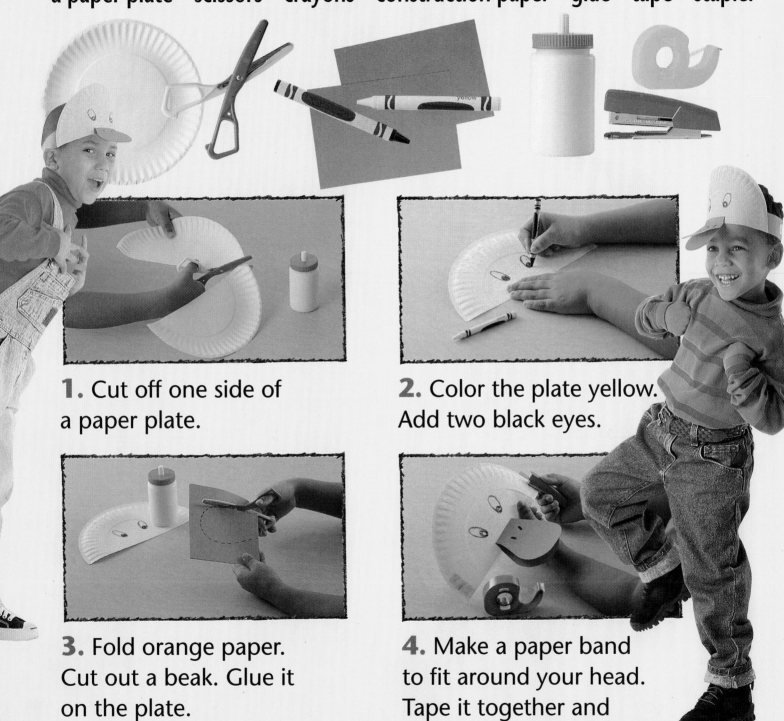

**1.** Cut off one side of a paper plate.

**2.** Color the plate yellow. Add two black eyes.

**3.** Fold orange paper. Cut out a beak. Glue it on the plate.

**4.** Make a paper band to fit around your head. Tape it together and staple it to the plate.

# Mom

# Me

Seals

Horses

Foxes

Sheep

Tigers

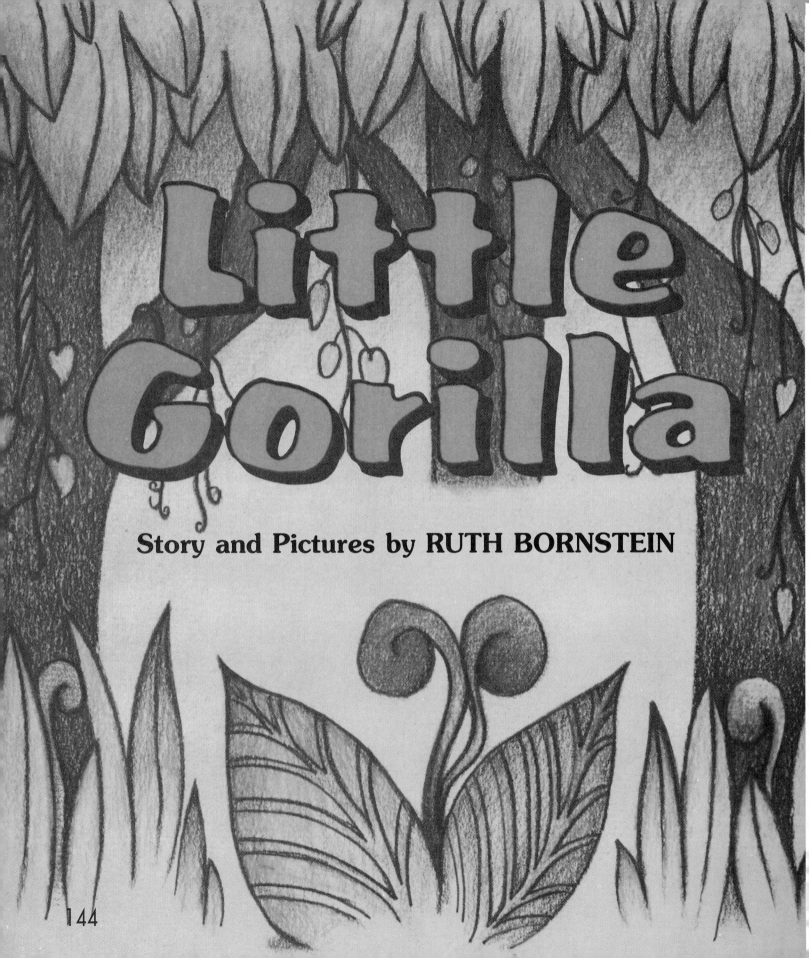

# Little Gorilla

## Story and Pictures by RUTH BORNSTEIN

Once there was a little gorilla,
and everybody loved him.

His mother loved him.

His father loved him.

His grandma and grandpa,
and his aunts and uncles loved him.

Even when he was only one day old,
everybody loved Little Gorilla.

**Pink Butterfly flying
through the forest,**

Green Parrot in his tree,
and Red Monkey in her tree,
all loved Little Gorilla.

**Even Big Boa Constrictor
thought Little Gorilla was nice.**

**Giraffe, walking tall through the forest,
was there when Little Gorilla needed him.**

Young Elephant, and Old Elephant too,
came to see him.

Lion roared his loudest roar for him.

**Even Old Hippo took him wherever he wanted
to go, because she loved Little Gorilla.**

Just about everybody in the great green
forest loved Little Gorilla!
Then one day something happened . . .

Little Gorilla began to grow

and Grow

and Grow

and GROW.

And one day,

# Little Gorilla was BIG!

**And everybody came,**

**and everybody sang**

"Happy Birthday
Little Gorilla!"

**And everybody still loved him.**

# Ruth Bornstein

"When I began writing and drawing pictures for books, I never told myself I was being silly. I used to paint little pictures of animals and flowers. Then I began writing words around the pictures. I just did what I felt. I didn't hold back. The best thing I can tell boys and girls who want to write and to draw is do what makes your heart sing."

# RESPONSE CORNER

## Little Gorilla's Birthday Card

It's Little Gorilla's birthday.
Let's make a gorilla-sized card for him.

### You will need:
a big sheet of paper

paints and brushes

crayons

masking tape

All the best!

We love you
Little
Gorilla

Happy Birth

**Acknowledgments**

For permission to reprint copyrighted material, grateful acknowledgment is made to the following sources:

*Clarion Books, a Houghton Mifflin Company imprint: Little Gorilla* by Ruth Bornstein. Copyright © 1976 by Ruth Bornstein. Cover illustration from *Five Little Monkeys Jumping on the Bed* by Eileen Christelow. Copyright © 1989 by Eileen Christelow.

*Dial Books for Young Readers, a division of Penguin Books USA Inc.:* Cover illustration by Lynne Russell from *One Smiling Grandma* by Ann Marie Linden. Illustration copyright © 1992 by Lynne Russell.

*Greenwillow Books, a division of William Morrow & Company, Inc.: Little Elephant* by Miela Ford, illustrated by Tana Hoban. Text copyright © 1994 by Miela Ford; photographs copyright © 1994 by Tana Hoban.

*Harcourt Brace & Company: Flower Garden* by Eve Bunting, illustrated by Kathryn Hewitt. Text copyright © 1994 by Eve Bunting; illustrations copyright © 1994 by Kathryn Hewitt. Cover illustration from *Vegetable Garden* by Douglas Florian. Copyright © 1991 by Douglas Florian.

*HarperCollins Publishers: Bet You Can't* by Penny Dale. Copyright © 1987 by Penny Dale.

*H. B. Holder, on behalf of Julie Holder:* "Where Did the Baby Go?" by Julie Holder. Text © 1987 by Julie Holder.

*Henry Holt and Company:* From *Five Little Ducks* by Ian Beck. Illustrations copyright © 1992 by Ian Beck.

*National Wildlife Federation:* "Bath Time" from *Your Big Backyard* Magazine, November 1993. Text copyright 1984 by the National Wildlife Federation. "Mom and Me" from *Your Big Backyard* Magazine, May 1993. Text copyright 1984 by the National Wildlife Federation.

*G. P. Putnam's Sons: An Egg Is An Egg* by Nicki Weiss. Copyright © 1990 by Monica J. Weiss.

*Viking Penguin, a division of Penguin Books USA Inc.:* Cover illustration by Kate Spohn from *Hide and Seek in the Yellow House* by Agatha Rose. Illustration copyright © 1992 by Kate Spohn.

**Photo Credits**

Key: (t) top, (b) bottom, (c) center.

Ron Kunzman/Harcourt Brace & Company,72, 84-85, 86-87; Steve Murez/Black Star/Harcourt Brace & Company, 84; Forest McMullin/Black Star/Harcourt Brace & Company, 85; David Levenson/Black Star/Harcourt Brace & Company, 139; Warren Faubel/Black Star/Harcourt Brace & Company, 165; John Johnson, 42-43,70-71, 122-125; Courtesy Walker Books Ltd., 67; Tana Hoban, 72-85,86; Dr. E. R. Degginger, Stephen J. Drasemann/DRK Photo, George H. Harrison, John H. Hoffman, 88-89; Fred Bruemmer, Wolfgang Bayer/Bruce Colman,Inc.,Silvester,142-143; Richard Hutchings, 166-167

**Illustration Credits**

Keith Baker, Cover Art; Peggy Tagel, 4-9; Nicki Weiss,10-41; Penny Dale,44-67; Julia Gorton, 68-69; Nathan Young Jarvis, 88-89; Kathryn Hewitt, 90-121; Ian Beck, 124-139; Ruth Bornstein, 144-165